# THE
# PROJECT
# MANAGER

## *LIFE IS A PROJECT*

# THE PROJECT MANAGER

## LIFE IS A PROJECT

Amy S. Hamilton, PMP

*The Project Manager: Life is a Project*
© 2017 by Amy S. Hamilton

While the author has made every effort to provide accurate internet addresses throughout the text, neither the publisher nor the author assumes any responsibility for errors, or for changes that occur after publication. Further, the author and publisher do not have any control over and do not assume any responsibility for third-party websites or their content.

ISBN-13: 978-0-9982746-2-1 (Hardcover)
ISBN-13: 978-0-9982746-3-8 (Softcover)
ISBN-13: 978-0-9982746-4-5 (E-book)

Edited by Jennifer Harshman, HarshmanServices.com
Cover Design and Interior Layout by James Woosley, FreeAgentPress.com

Published by Free Agent Press, FreeAgentPress.com
Satsuma, Alabama 36572
VID: 20170420

# Dedication

*In memory of my father,*
*who purchased a*
*Brother Word Processor 500*
*for me when I started university*
*and encouraged me to write.*

*To my friends and family;*
*I will not list them as I will forget someone*
*and they will be cross with me.*

# CONTENTS

# FOREWORD

## *by James B. Woosley, PMP*

---

**IF LIFE IS A PROJECT,** then we are all project managers. Some of us are great at all aspects of it, while others have genius for one area and idiocy for another. Sadly, some are blind to the fact that they are in charge of their most important project: their own life.

I didn't really know what project management was until I joined the Air Force. I remember being a young lieutenant and hearing a friend planning to study for the Project Management Professional exam. Something about those words and the letters "PMP" were shiny enough to excite me. Then I learned about the hours of experience and massive test required and the idea seemed impossible.

Six years later, the excitement was rekindled when becoming a PMP was an unspoken requirement in the consulting company I worked for after leaving the service. I had a few years under my belt, some training on the horizon, and the $400 exam fee would be reimbursed if I passed (always a bonus!).

I took charge and organized a study group. There were 10 or 12 of us who met regularly, some fellow consultants and some clients. We met twice a week for about eight weeks, then the testing began. One by one, we all passed the exam and added "PMP" to our resumes and business cards.

In the years that followed, I managed many projects, both big and small, personal and professional. I can see that the concept of life being a project was just out of reach all that time. It didn't become a tangible concept or solid thought until I read the book you now hold in your hands.

This is not a fancy book. It's not about a grand story or a set of instructions you can follow to instantly live a better or more efficient life. It's not a how-to book and it's certainly not just motivational fluff.

This book is a spark. It's a little arc of electricity aimed at the dormant-but-fertile fields of your mind. If you allow it to strike, it will set you on a journey to projectize your life.

It doesn't matter if you're blind to what project management is or have decades of experience, degrees, and certifications. Unless you wake up to the fact that you are in charge of your life, you can't get the most out of it. At worst, you're on a sinking ship wondering where the captain is, oblivious to the fancy uniform you're wearing. At best, you'll have accidental success. As for me? I want more than accidental successs.

Enjoy the read and the spark it can provide.

**— James B. Woosley, PMP**
Author of *Conquer the Entrepreneur's Kryptonite*
and *Challenge Accepted!*

# SELECTED

---

**"LIFE IS A PROJECT" THE** tagline read, under Thomas Robert Morgan's email signature block.

Ashley stared at the computer and couldn't believe her eyes. She blinked twice and then reread the email. She had been selected as the IT integration manager for the new smart building, which her company, InTech, was a subcontractor for in downtown Denver. She wanted to get up and scream and dance with delight, but of course refrained because she was in her office. It was a dream opportunity and she had worked her whole career for that moment.

"What are you smiling at?" her coworker Chris asked, standing in the doorway to her office, leaning casually. Chris was the youngest member of their office team and often came across as an eager puppy.

"I just found out that I was selected for the new Denver building," Ashley told him, not able to hold back the excitement in her voice, but also not wanting to hurt Chris's feelings.

"That's great for you," Chris said, trying to hide his own disappointment. "I guess that means I'll get to help the next rich kid who wants to upgrade a condo with Daddy's money."

"Hey," Ashley said, getting up and crossing the room toward Chris. "Rich kids who want smart condos pay our bills. I know how much you wanted this position, but only one of us could get selected. Besides, I'm senior to you," she added.

Running her hand through her hair, she dreaded having to tell the third IT integration manager the news. "We should probably go tell Mark, together." Mark was the unofficial lead for their team and had worked at InTech several years longer than both of them.

Chris smiled. "If I had to lose, better to you than Mark. That guy would never let me live it down." Chris and Mark treated each other with good-natured rivalry.

"You are both great integration managers," Ashley

said with a smile, walking past him into the hallway toward Mark's office. "I just happen to be better." She threw a sidelong glance over her shoulder and walked a little faster.

The three of them got along very well most of the time and often traded ideas and swapped projects. It wasn't often that a state-of-the-art smart office building came along as a project. Most of the projects InTech did for smart IT integration were in fact condos for young, rich kids. They often wanted a completely integrated system with all the bells and whistles to impress their friends. Sometimes it reminded Ashley of the old movies that tried to depict a futuristic "pad" where some young playboy could make a bed appear out of the wall, classic jazz music pour forth, and colorful lights set the mood with a click of a button. Some of their clients even had their places featured on reality television shows.

"What's up, guys?" Mark asked as the two of them barged into his office.

"Ashley beat us both out of the Denver building," Chris blurted before Ashley had time to speak.

"Better her than you," Mark responded with a good-natured laugh. He always enjoyed giving Chris a hard time, like a kid brother.

"That's basically what he said," Ashley responded, pointing at Chris.

"Let's go out after work for drinks to celebrate your good fortune," Chris said. Being the younger, single guy, this was always his go-to celebration option. "I am so jealous that you get to work with Thomas Robert Morgan."

"I can't tonight," Mark said. "My oldest is running in her last track meet of the season and it's her senior year."

"Ashley?" Chris questioned, raising an eyebrow.

"Just one and only if we go across the street to the café. I have a book-club meeting at 6:30," she said, adding the new commitment into her phone. She was so grateful for her phone calendar. She was always trying to squeeze in just one more item into her busy day, too often trying to sort out competing activities and sometimes failing to do so.

"Perfect," Chris said. "I'll stop by your office at 5:00 sharp." Chris knew he would have to pry Ashley away from the keyboard to get her out on time.

Ashley paused before leaving and asked, "Mark, are you sure you are okay with this? You are the senior IT integration manager here."

"I'm fine with it. I am really trying to spend some more time with my family. My oldest is graduating high school this year and the second is only two years behind. If I don't put my family first now, when I will I have the time?" He could see the look of doubt hadn't left Ashley's face and added, "When I was asked about this a few months ago, before the company even won the bid, I recommended you for this role. You are detail oriented and dedicated to your job. You deserve this opportunity."

"Thanks, Mark," Ashley beamed back. "I appreciate the vote of confidence. It is so great working with you and Chris."

The rest of the day went by quickly and before she knew it, Chris was standing over her desk at exactly five o'clock. "Time to leave," he said, giving her a boyish grin.

"Just a few more minutes to finish this email," Ashley replied, glancing up.

Chris stood in the doorway impatiently, making as much noise as possible in quite a comical way. At 29, he was clinging to the still-under-30 mantra. He loved to tease his two older coworkers that they were so much older than he was.

"It's already 5:10," he sighed, pointing to his wrist, which didn't have a watch on it. Chris loved to make fun of Ashley and Mark, who still wore traditional wrist-watches instead of relying on their smart phones.

"Ready," Ashley said, "but don't forget: one drink and then I have to slide over to the Indian food restaurant next door to meet my book club."

After her single celebratory drink with Chris, she left the bar of the café and joined her book-club friends for a lively discussion on the book *Sense and Sensibility*. By the time she finally got home, she was worn out and Cupcake was waiting at the door. Seeing the large Rhodesian Ridgeback always brought a smile to her face. She quickly grabbed his leash and took him for a short walk around the neighborhood. She was exhausted as she went to bed and promised that over the weekend she would reexamine her schedule so that she could exercise and spend more time with Cupcake. Of course, she made that same promise to herself almost every night before bed.

When she woke up in the morning, she instinctively reached across the bed before she groggily remembered that Stephen had moved out almost two months ago. She still hadn't told anyone at work or even her friends that he most likely wasn't coming back. She still needed to get him removed from the household bills. One more to thing to add to her list of things to think about over the weekend. Cupcake whined impatiently from the foot of the bed and she knew she had best get up and walk him right away. A Rhodesian Ridgeback could make quite a puddle if he didn't get out in time to do his business.

As Ashley walked Cupcake around the block, she thought about the upcoming project. She was really excited about this opportunity and felt like she needed the change. She had heard so many great stories about the project manager that she couldn't wait for the kickoff meeting.

# THE KICKOFF
# MEETING

**THOMAS ROBERT MORGAN WAS KNOWN** as the best large-project manager for smart buildings in the industry. He was level headed, detail oriented, but most importantly, he knew how to bring a team together. He was known for his ability to work with the high-technology engineers who tried to show off how smart they were to the creative architects who sometimes became overly creative and forgot that there were deadlines. He had been the project lead for buildings in many high-tech Asian cities, including Shanghai and Singapore.

He looked around the conference room at the team, which he had hand selected for the Denver building. This building was by far going to be the most advanced smart building in the region and he needed this project to meet all the key milestones and avoid any delays or cost overruns. His serious, penetrating gaze met each set of eyes; he knew that taking his time and setting the stage at a kickoff meeting was critical to the future success of his team. He had learned through trial and error in the past that not having a strong kickoff could derail a project from the start.

"Team," Thomas began with his bass voice and slight Alabama drawl, "I handpicked each one of you either because I worked with you before or by your reputation and resume. I need *every* individual on this team to realize that this is a team and no longer a room of individuals with unique skill sets." He paused to look around the room and connect with each set of eyes. He had played football for Alabama and had almost gone to the NFL. He was keenly aware of how to use his physicality to his advantage. "If the architects fail, we all fail. If the construction workers fail, we all fail. If the technology fails, we all fail. I will not tolerate team members who point fingers or shift blame, is that clear?" he asked, looking each of the assembled leads in the eye. He noticed which ones looked away and which held his gaze.

"We have an aggressive timeline, but I know that this team can pull it off. I will be holding a weekly project meeting with the members in this room," he looked around at his hand-selected team. "Before we get started with project details, however, I want you to get to know each other." He heard a few groans from around the table.

"As long as we don't have to get naked and play bongo drums in the woods," Troy the construction manager shouted. That earned a few laughs and broke some of the tension in the room. Thomas had worked with Troy on several projects in the past. He appreciated his humor almost as much as his work ethic.

"Well, Troy," Thomas drawled, "it looks like you are our first volunteer. Please share with the team your name, role on the project team, favorite sports team, and the worst project you have worked on and why."

"The last one is the easiest," Troy laughed. "The first project I worked for Thomas on was brutal. He took over our failing project in Shanghai that was already six months behind and significantly over budget. Of course, when the great Thomas Robert Morgan took over the project, things got a lot better, quickly. That is why I have followed Thomas around the world and why I am on this project now," he took a deep breath and looked around the room. "For those of you who I haven't worked with before, I am Troy Davis, the construction manager for this project." He noticed Thomas still looking at him and added, "As for sports, I'll cheer for any team that is trying to beat Alabama in any sport." That earned a chuckle from around the room.

"Hey, gang, I'm Terri Lewis," a small woman said and smiled at the group. "I am responsible for Human Resources, so as we move through the project, I will be doing the hiring for the team and taking care of any benefits and other HR issues for you. I have worked with Thomas for several years and can't say that I have ever had a bad project. I'm fortunate to have left a medium-sized operations background to come work for Mr. Morgan on his projects. I am a Dallas fan," she added, earning a few good-natured boos from around the room.

"I'm Jason Lee, not the actor even though I'm as good looking," he joked to the group. "I am responsible for contracting, so I am everyone's new best friend," he smiled at the crew. "Everyone always teases me, but I really don't follow sports; I am a huge fan of mixed martial arts, which is totally cliché. The worst project I was ever on was before I met Thomas and I wish he had been there to save us. Nobody communicated with their fellow team members and the project was never completed. It was a tough lesson for me to learn," he added on a serious note.

"I'm the building architect for this project, Jim Brown, and I'll try not to be too much a prima donna." He smiled at Thomas and then the rest of the team. "This is my first time working with Thomas Robert Morgan. My worst project was a few years ago when I had significant issues with the construction manager on my project and we just couldn't get along. The PM didn't resolve the issues and we continued to get further off schedule and over budget. Eventually the project was completed, but all parties were dissatisfied with the final result." Seeing the serious looks around the room, he added, "We never had a meeting like this to kick off the project and just meeting the entire team makes me feel like this project has a lot more hope. My favorite sports team is the Red Wings, so I won't be too popular here in Avalanche country," he added with a chuckle.

"I'm the most hated man on any project team, Carl Nelson," a man with an expensive suit told the group seated around the table. "I have worked with Thomas Robert Morgan on several projects and he keeps me around because I am the best lawyer he has ever worked with." Carl laughed.

"Saying you are the best lawyer I ever worked with is hardly a compliment," Thomas responded. "You are, after all, still a lawyer." Everyone laughed at their banter and could see that they had a positive energy between them.

"The worst project I was ever on was almost ten years ago. We were behind schedule and nobody would listen when I told them the issues with zoning and the city planning commission. The next project I was on was with our PM here." He pointed to Thomas. "Now I won't work on a project unless he is the PM or unless he personally vouches for the PM. I shamelessly admit to being a New England Patriots fan." This last earned him a few good-natured hisses.

"I'm Ashley Baker and responsible for IT integration," Ashley said quickly, realizing that she was now the only person who hadn't introduced themselves yet. "It is my first time working directly with Thomas, but we have done some virtual work for him in the past. The worst project I was on was a small integration project for a young man in Aspen who kept changing the scope of what he wanted. His father was rather indulgent, so luckily the cost never became an issue. It was just very frustrating for the project team and we were almost six months late in delivery. I'm a native to the area," she added, "so I support all teams Denver."

Thomas smiled at Ashley. "That concludes my team of direct reports on the project. Some of your direct reports will be working closely with each other and everyone should get the opportunity to mingle at this evening's social. I believe that interacting at the human level is an important element to project success. Before you bring a conflict to me regarding another team member, you need to have exhausted courses of action between yourself and the other person. As I've already indicated, I will not tolerate back stabbing. If you have a fear of confronting people about work problems, this isn't a team you want to be a part of. You can let me know after the kickoff meeting whether this is or is not the right team for you." Around the room there were some nervous looks, but Thomas could tell that everyone wanted to be there.

"For the rest of the meeting, we will be covering the project charter and the scope of the project. I know all of you have worked on projects before, but not all of you have worked with me. Everything you do from this day forward will be based on the project charter and scope. When you ask me a design question, I will ask you, 'How does this impact the triple constraint: cost, time, quality?' If you ask me an IT integration question, I will ask you, 'How does this impact cost, time, quality?' If you take an extra ten minutes for lunch, ask yourself, 'How does this impact cost, time, quality? Seeing the pattern?" It was obvious who had worked with him on a project before because they were all smiling and nodding. The members new to the team looked a little surprised. Thomas continued, "It is my belief that projects end up over budget, running late, and not meeting project quality expectations because the management team forgets the basics. I am here to remind you of the basics."

**Scope** *or the* **triple constraint** *consists of cost/resources, time/schedule and quality/product. The rule of thumb is you can get only two out of the three.*

The rest of the meeting continued with Thomas presenting the details of the project charter and his expectations of the management team. After the meeting, Ashley felt she had a better understanding of the project than any project she had ever been a part of before. She was looking forward to the next year, working as a part of this team. Each of the members of this project team seemed genuinely excited to be a part of the project.

"Project Management is both an art and a science," he concluded to his team. "I need you to manage each of your respective areas within the triple constraint, the science part. However, I also need you to be flexible and creative; that is the art part."

As Thomas expected, none of the members from his new project team approached him about their compatibility with their new team. A few of the members had expressed concerns about his requirement that members work out of a central location at least three days a week instead of teleworking from their corporate offices or their homes, but he had found that being in the same physical space encouraged collaboration and interaction amongst team members. He was a firm believer that understanding the scope and communications between his direct reports were the keys to the successful record he had of completing projects that were on time, within budget, and up to specifications.

# SCHEDULE
# CONFLICTS

**ASHLEY WAS FIGHTING BUMPER-TO-BUMPER TRAFFIC** after work, in the dry summer of Denver. She needed to get to her house to pick up Cupcake and then drive to her mom's birthday party. Her sister Brittany had arranged everything and would be there with her family. Brittany's husband Jake was a doctor and they had two kids: Jared, who was eight, and Jessica, who had just turned six). Her father, a retired army officer, had passed away from a sudden heart attack the year prior and the sisters had made a pact to spend more time with their mother.

Ashley knew that Brittany was frustrated because she was often the one arranging family get-togethers. Ashley wanted to spend more time with her family, but work and social obligations were always a struggle for her. That day was no exception. She finally pulled into her driveway and rushed into the house to convince Cupcake that he wanted to go for a ride. She knew that it wasn't fair to the poor dog to leave him alone so much and despite the extra driving time, he would enjoy family time as much as the two-legged members of the family would.

When Ashley showed up at her mother's house, her sister and her family were already there. Both Jared and Jessica rushed outside to greet her and Cupcake. They gave hugs to their Auntie Ashley and their Cousin Cupcake. Brittany disapproved of the children giving the title of "cousin" to a dog, but had given up on breaking them of this habit.

After dinner and birthday cake, the three women sat down to try to schedule some upcoming family time. On almost any date suggested by the other two, Ashley already had an engagement on her calendar, which she consulted with her phone app.

"This is why Stephen moved out," Brittany chided her sister. "You never made time for him."

"That's not why Stephen moved out," Ashley countered, but knew that it was partly true.

"Stephen moved out because you two should never have been living like a married couple before you were married," her mother stated flatly. Gloria Dean Baker had done her best to raise her two daughters in a Christian household and the fact that they were grown adults and living on their own never prevented her from letting her daughters know when she thought they were wrong. She was her daughters' greatest supporter and their greatest critic.

"Let's focus on finding some dates that work so we can all get together," Ashley suggested, wanting to take the focus away from her failed relationship. "When does summer break end for the kids?" she asked.

After setting up some days to get back together with her family over the next few months, it was time to head home. The family exchanged hugs all around with Jared and Jessica being bribed with promises of leftover birthday cake as in incentive to allow Cupcake to get loaded into Ashley's Jeep.

When she checked her phone before leaving to drive home, she was reminded that she was supposed to meet a few of her girlfriends for drinks. She was exhausted and decided to call and cancel. She had a tendency to overbook her calendar; she canceled out on evenings like this a little too often. She reflected that she should never have overcommitted in the first place.

During the drive home, Ashley contemplated her overbooked schedule and wondered how she could streamline things to have more free time. She constantly rearranged her schedule and when she attended events like her nieces and nephews' school plays, she was distracted, because she knew she had another event immediately following. It wasn't fair to poor Cupcake to be left home alone and despite the fact that she was paying a dog-nanny service, she knew the dog wasn't getting enough attention.

When she got home, she walked Cupcake around the block one last time before settling in for the night. She really did need to organize her personal life a little better. Her overbooked schedule left her exhausted and feeling stressed. She also knew that her eating and exercise habits needed to improve, but who had time for cooking and working out?

# Two Offices is One Too Many

---

ONCE THE PROJECT GOT UNDERWAY, Ashley was spending at least three days a week at the smart-building project office, which Thomas Robert Morgan had mandated, and the other two days at the InTech office with Mark and Chris. Balancing time between the two offices should have become routine after a month, but Ashley was still struggling.

Sometimes she considered working solely out of the new project office, but she felt she needed to spend time at InTech to bounce ideas off Mark and Chris in order to keep abreast of changes in IT integration. Her new colleagues were from very diverse fields and she might not hear about new innovations in the industry if she didn't make time to work out of the InTech office. The new project team had really come together since the kickoff meeting, but architecture and construction were not IT. She simply didn't feel the same about the new project office; in many ways, InTech felt like home.

Chris came by her office after lunch, still in his workout clothes. "I thought you were going to start working out during lunch," he said, standing in her doorway.

"I have been spending time between offices for almost two months and can barely manage it," she told Chris. "I just can't add gym time to my already crazy schedule."

"You're the one who keeps telling me that you want to get fitter," he reminded her. "Studies show that your physical fitness is directly linked to the other aspects of your life," Chris added, knowing that Ashley loved hard data. After her father had passed away from a heart attack the year before, she had promised to take better care of her health.

Mark stopped by the door, having heard part of the conversation. "Even if you don't have time for a full workout, just getting out and walking around the park has great health benefits."

"Great, the two of you are ganging up on me." She glared. "I'm going to start working every day at the new project office," she mock threatened.

"You wouldn't do that," Mark replied confidently. "You know that without your presence here a few days a week to act as the middle sibling, Chris and I wouldn't survive."

"Besides, you need to get an IT fix with us geeks. You'll never get that hanging out with your 'Starchitect' and his muddy-boot construction workers," Chris added.

"Fine," Ashley capitulated, "I'll keep coming by and I know that I need to get my schedule under control and better organized to work at two offices."

"At least you are showered," Mark pointed out.

"Fine," Chris said. "I can take a hint." He walked away, presumably to shower and change for the rest of the day.

"Let me know if you need any help getting organized," Mark told her. "When my daughters hit high school, I realized I needed to examine my work–life balance. I didn't want to miss out on my last few years of having them at home."

"Thanks, Mark," Ashley said. "I appreciate the offer. Sometimes I just feel so overwhelmed, I am not even sure where to begin. Now that I am working out of two offices, I feel more stressed than ever. Sometimes, I even leave from working all day at one office to go to the other office for a few hours."

"Ashley," Mark said seriously, "as your friend, I'm going to give you some advice. You can't do everything. You are eventually going to have to set some priorities or you will end up with serious health issues. I know firsthand." Mark took a deep breath and added, "Martha threatened to leave me and take the girls if I couldn't make them a priority."

"Wow," Ashley responded in disbelief. "I know that had to be a shock." Ashley knew Mark was a dedicated husband and father.

"It woke me up," Mark confessed. "Now, I spend a lot of effort ensuring that my work does not become more important than my family."

"Thanks, Mark," Ashley replied, knowing that she really did need to reconsider her work–life balance.

# THE
# CONVERSATION

---

ASHLEY SAT AT HER DESK in the smart-building
project office, surrounded by cartons of Chinese take-
out, trying to finalize a few tasks before leaving for the
weekend. Thomas Robert Morgan stopped outside her
door, wearing a track suit, and paused. "Getting ready
for the weekend?" he asked.

"Just finishing a few emails and updating the project schedule on the portal," she told him.

"Mind if I come in for a minute?" he asked. Not waiting for an answer, he dropped into a chair opposite her desk with a grace that was surprising for a man his age and size. He was certainly more physically fit than she was, despite being the same age as her father would have been.

"When I played for Alabama, everyone thought I would be a professional football player," he began, highlighting his physical fitness as if he had read her mind. "Despite aspirations for the NFL, I wanted to have a real education in case something went wrong. That is why I wanted to be a business major, unlike a lot of my teammates." He paused a moment. "I had seen and heard of too many guys who got injured or washed out. I wanted a fallback plan."

"I fell in love with project management during my first class. I found that the principles of project management could be applied to the personal aspects of my life. My very limited finances in college; my difficulty struggling with practice, classes, and socializing; and most important: the outcomes in my life. If I hadn't found project management, I don't know what I would have done when I blew out my knee my senior year. I was lucky that I had another vocation that was calling to me." Thomas paused, waiting to see Ashley's reaction to his very open disclosure on how he had come into project management.

"You have a reputation for being one of the best project managers in the industry," Ashley told him.

"I have been fortunate in my career," he told her. "I am in a profession that I love and that I am able to apply in my everyday life. Have you ever thought about that, Ashley?" Thomas Robert Morgan looked at her intently as he asked this question.

"I know that being selected to work for you on this project was very competitive and that I am very grateful for this opportunity." Ashley wasn't sure exactly where the conversation was leading. Was Mr. Morgan disappointed with some area of her work? What did he mean by applying project management to everyday life?

He resumed his story from college. "When I had my first project-management class, I realized, 'Life is a project.' The definition of a project according to the *Project Management Body of Knowledge*, or the PMBOK, is 'It's a temporary endeavor undertaken to create a unique product, service, or result.' When I first learned that, I thought, 'Wow, Life is a Project!'"

Ashley wasn't sure where exactly Mr. Morgan was headed with his story, but somehow felt that it was important for to her to understand. "How exactly is life a project?" she asked, not completely seeing things the same way as her project manager. She was a certified project manager, but she couldn't recall any references to life being defined as a project when she studied for her exam.

Thomas had put a lot of thought into project management over the length of his career and was able to unpack his concept of "life as a project" with an almost Zen-like simplicity. "Every project has a beginning and an end; every life has a beginning and an end." He paused to let it soak in. "Every project creates something unique and every life is unique. Therefore, every life is a project," he concluded, smiling.

Ashley was almost blown away by the simplicity of this concept. Was it really true? Was her life a project? Could the same skills she used at work assist her with getting her day-to-day life organized? She had never thought about it in such a way. Could it really be this simple? She had been struggling with her personal life for so long. Did she already have the keys to success and just not know it?

Thomas could see from Ashley's face that she was processing this concept. "When I watch you at work, I see an amazing project manager with a lot of potential. What I worry about is that you don't appear to be using your skills outside of these four walls."

Ashley felt a little defensive and vulnerable, but had

to ask, "What do you see, Mr. Morgan?" She hesitated. "Where do you think I need to improve?"

"I don't want to overstep my bounds, Ashley," Thomas Robert Morgan told her. "I want you to know, first, that I think you are doing a great job as the lead for IT integration and that your job is secure. This conversation is based on my observations this past month. I would like to share my theory with you a bit more, but only if you want to hear about it," he told her.

"Mr. Morgan," Ashley said, "I have felt overwhelmed for a long time. I try not to show it at work and to be a professional. I enjoy working on this project." She hesitated but added, "If your theory could help me outside of the workplace, I would like to know what you see."

"I see someone who is organized, task driven, a wonderful communicator, scheduler, budgeter, and team player in the office," he began. "Outside of work, I see a woman who is always running between events and who isn't able to reach her personal goals. I see someone who doesn't use the triple constraint to focus her life outside of the office."

Ashley nodded. "Thanks for your insight, Mr. Morgan." She always felt overwhelmed in her personal life. She had too much to do and there was never enough time or money to do it all well. She was constantly promising herself that she would get organized.

She also felt slightly embarrassed. She always tried to appear professional and under control at work. She wasn't very happy that a famous project manager like Thomas Robert Morgan had observed this about her.

"I have had to struggle with the same issues in my life," he told her reassuringly. "People often refer to work–life balance and there are all kinds of techniques to address this area," he told her. "I have just found that as a project manager, we already have the tools. We just need to learn how to adjust and apply them."

"Please, go on," Ashley encouraged, leaning forward. She had been struggling with this area for so long and it felt like Thomas Robert Morgan was throwing her a life preserver.

"When I make decisions in my personal life," Thomas went on, "I use the triple constraint to help me to determine what is important. Everything in life has a cost; it may not always be financial. Your time is a precious and limited resource in your life. You should only be doing things that truly add value," he said, driving the concept home.

"That is why you are such a good project manager," Ashley said, "because you think of the triple constraint all of the time. This is the first project I have ever worked on where all the team members are constantly analyzing the impact to cost, schedule, and quality."

"I'm not surprised," Thomas said a little sadly, shaking his head. "We all learn about the triple constraint to get certified, but often project managers don't hold steadily to it in projects. Think about how smoothly a project can go when you focus every day on the impact of the triple constraint." He held her gaze and added, "How much more would you accomplish in your personal life if you applied the same principle?"

Ashley smiled at the thought. "During the kickoff meeting, you really emphasized the need to always consider the impact to the triple constraint. Is that why you are such a successful project manager?" She continued to focus on project management at work and hadn't quite shifted into how it could be used in her daily life.

Thomas thought a moment and replied, "I believe that it helps me to be a good project manager, but it helps me more in my own life management. Having a wife and two boys has always kept me busy. It is a little easier now that my sons have grown up and graduated college, but before that it was crazy hectic. My first grandchild was born last year and that has added a new dynamic as well," he paused, scrutinizing Ashley for a reaction.

After seeing a flicker of understanding, he continued, "When I have to make a decision in my personal life, I apply the triple constraint. For example, visiting my son for the birth of his child, that was easy. The value far outweighed any cost incurred or time spent. Does that make sense?" he asked her.

"Yes," she replied, seeing the logic behind his decision from a project-management perspective. "But wouldn't most people just call that common sense?"

Thomas realized that Ashley needed a less obvious example, one that she could relate to a bit more. "The reason I go running after work is also because of the triple constraint," he informed her. "I could try to fight Denver I-25 traffic, but I probably wouldn't make it home much sooner than I do now. Instead, I take about forty-five minutes after work and complete a nice jog during peak rush hour. By doing my run before going home, I'm able to maximize the triple constraint. Do you see how this is?" he asked Ashley.

"Sort of," she responded. "Of the three constraints, time is the most obvious. You spend less time driving and if you were going to work out for forty-five minutes regardless, you have more time overall," she reasoned.

"That is correct," Thomas responded, pleased to see her understanding. "What about the other two constraints?"

"Well," Ashley thought aloud, "you probably get more value from a run than sitting in traffic and if you were in traffic, it might cause you stress and you might have less value overall."

"Great," Thomas encouraged. "What about cost?"

"You probably save money on gas by not sitting idle on the highway and it would be less wear and tear on your car," she added.

"That's good, Ashley," Thomas Robert Morgan praised her, "but what about the opportunity cost? By switching my schedule, I am maximizing my opportunity to run, while minimizing my opportunity to sit in traffic and all the negative health and environmental aspects associated with it." He realized he needed to put this back into a work project, which Ashley could easily understand. "For your work projects, you do a great job of this already. You just need to consider how you could apply this beyond work."

Ashley smiled. "That makes so much sense! It is just basic scoping."

Thomas returned her enthusiasm. "Now you see how anything, even something as simple as my run and commute schedule, can be impacted by project-management techniques." He looked at her seriously. "Over the past month on this project, I have observed that you do a great job of applying project-management techniques at work. I just wonder if maybe you might be able to benefit from using some of these techniques in your personal life," he added.

"Sir," Ashley responded, "I really appreciate your time and this is an entirely new way for me to consider project management. Would you mind if I talk to you again after trying to 'scope' some of my life?" she asked.

Thomas realized that the seed was planted and it would take a while to grow. "I would really enjoy working with you on your life as a project," he told her. "I've been at the business of applying PM techniques to everyday life for a long time. I actually call it 'Projectizing your Lifestyle,'" he told her with a laugh.

"That's catchy," Ashley said. "I guess that I need to wrap up for the evening and when I get home, I am going to look at areas where I can 'Projectize my Lifestyle.'"

"Great," Thomas responded. "I look forward to hearing your progress." He left Ashley's office smiling. He couldn't wait to go home and tell his wife about his newest protégé.

When Ashley arrived home, she immediately took Cupcake out for his nightly walk. Cupcake was certainly very high when it came to value in her life, but she knew she wasn't spending enough time with him. How could she adjust other areas of her life, like Mr. Morgan did with his commute and exercise schedule, she wondered. That night when she went to bed, she didn't feel quite as overwhelmed about her life. She was a good project manager; all she had to do was scope her lifestyle.

# LIFE
# IS A PROJECT

---

**THAT WEEKEND, ASHLEY DID SOMETHING** she had been promising to do for a long time. She set aside a few hours to look at her day-to-day life and determine what she was spending so much time doing and how she could better scope her activities. She was constantly moving her schedule around to accommodate activities and knew that she needed to review which ones were truly priorities and which ones were not worth the cost.

In addition to the element of time, she needed to consider the other two areas of the triple constraint. She needed to consider the costs and resources applied to activities. She also needed to place an emphasis on the value of an activity.

She began creating a separate list of her priorities. Then she could answer the critical question: Was she in fact spending her time and money on her priorities?

She came up with a short list of priorities that were very general:

☐ Family (to include Cupcake)

☐ Relationships (friends and social acquaintances)

☐ Self-development

☐ Charity work

☐ Health and fitness

After writing out a list of her priorities, she started to go through each of the next month's scheduled activities. She tried to categorize each activity under her five areas of priorities. She quickly realized that even though her family was listed as her number-one priority, she was spending the least amount of time on that priority. She also realized that she spent a lot of time on a category that she hadn't put as a priority: entertainment. Some activities were easy to place in a category, like her monthly meeting for the local Project Management

Institute chapter, clearly self-development. For activities like book club, she could stretch it to self-development, but movie night with the girls was clearly entertainment.

She decided that there were some activities which she could cut out without having a significant negative impact on her priorities. This included movies with friends. She realized that movies took up a lot of time and that she wasn't even able to talk to her friends during the film. She normally spent time with her friends after the movie to catch up. It would be better to go out to dinner or have a cup of coffee with a friend. By doing this, she would reduce the cost by not paying for a movie, which normally included movie snacks as well, and even if they still talked for hours, she would reduce the time spent by an hour and half if she eliminated the movie. She would also increase the value because instead of discussing the fictitious life of movie characters, she would discuss the real life of her friends.

Another activity which she felt she could rearrange was passive time with her friends, like trivia night. A few of her friends were part of a walking group on the same night. Instead of eating nachos and drinking calorie-laden drinks, she could spend more time with Cupcake and add a little physical activity to her schedule. She decided that this was a good choice within the triple constraint. She had placed health and fitness in her top five priorities, but none of her weekly activities included this priority.

She needed to ensure that her activities outside of work added value to her life and that the cost and time out of her day were worth it. Reviewing her activities made her realize that she was doing a lot of things out of habit, not considering the triple constraint. She would also need to become stronger at saying "No" to activities that did not meet the triple constraint. This would be a challenge for her.

She reviewed her project reports every Monday to determine the project activities that needed her attention each week. She realized she needed to apply the same diligence in her personal life; she was determined that each Sunday night she would review her personal activities. She would ensure her scheduled activities reflected her personal priorities and bind them by the triple constraint. She realized that Thomas Robert Morgan was right: Life is a Project.

# Personal Life Project Kick-off

**Ashley was excited to have** an opportunity to apply her project-management skills to her day-to-day life. Because her daily life was a little more streamlined, she noticed she was able to enjoy her time with Cupcake and her family. She couldn't wait to talk to Thomas Robert Morgan, but he was out of town on a business trip for the week. She went through with her identified schedule changes and took Cupcake on his first group walk that Thursday. While catching up with her friend Sonya during the walk, she realized that she was very tired and out of breath.

"After our walk is finished, we gather at the smoothie bar," Sonya told her. "It has a covered outdoor area where the dogs are able to hang out, even when it gets cold."

"Thanks," Ashley said. "I think I will stay and check it out."

Sonya introduced Ashley to some of the other members of the group when they finished their 5k walk. Ashley was tired, but the energy smoothie she purchased was better than any nachos she had ever had on trivia night. It was great to be able to spend time and meet people while also doing something that was good for her. Cupcake enjoyed meeting the other dogs and receiving the attention of all the strangers coming up to pet him.

That weekend, instead of spending Friday night at the movies, she took Cupcake over to her sister Brittany's house to spend some time with Jared and Jessica. The kids were super excited to spend some time in the backyard with the dog, while the sisters were able to catch up. Ashley told Brittany about her conversation with her project manager and her plan to use her project-management skills to scope her life. After listening to her for a while, Brittany had an idea.

"You know how crazy our lives are around the holidays. Maybe you could use these techniques to help us get a bit more organized at that time of the year, too."

"Projectize Your Holidays," Ashley exclaimed. "I like it. Let's work on this later, after I get a chance to think about it for a while." After all, it was only late summer and there would be plenty of time to get around to this later, she thought.

She then met up with her movie-night friends at their usual spot where they hung out after the movie. Because it was summer, they had reserved an outdoor table and Ashley could bring Cupcake along. The ladies declared that the movie wasn't very good and they quickly moved on to topics to which Ashley could contribute and she joined in on the conversation. Ashley was very excited to share with her friends her new approach to getting her life better organized and they shared some thoughts and tips with her on what worked for them. Some of them seemed intrigued by the idea; most of them were struggling with too many activities and not enough time to do them all. Instead of feeling drained at the end of the week and promising that the next week would go better, she felt energized and was wondering what other project-management techniques could be applied to her daily life.

Despite not having had a formal project kickoff meeting, Ashley felt like her "Life is a Project" kickoff had gone well. She had effectively communicated her new views with both her family members and friends.

She had also started to apply the triple constraint to her daily activities. When she reflected on her week, she realized that she couldn't remember a time when she had managed her activities so well. She knew that there was still a lot to do, but instead of feeling overwhelmed, she felt optimistic.

# A WBS
# FOR THE GYM

**THE NEXT WEEK, SHE WAS** excited to share her new insights with her project manager. The idea of using her PM skills and applying them to her personal life had never occurred to her, but it made so much sense. She was going to look for Thomas Robert Morgan, but as usual, her boss and mentor seemed like he was able to read her mind.

Thomas stopped by Ashley's desk at the end of the day and he could see that she was brimming with energy. "How is scoping your personal life going?"

"Great," she responded with enthusiasm, and told him some of what she had been able to accomplish.

"Sounds like you are totally embracing the concept," he told her with a smile. "Not everyone does. Do you have any questions?"

"I have one question for you." She hesitated. "But it might seem silly."

"There's no such thing as a stupid question," he chuckled, giving her the old quote. "Go ahead and ask."

"I am having a lot of difficulty trying to adjust my schedule so that I have time to work out. It isn't just trying to make time in my day, but bringing workout clothes, taking a shower, and changing for my next activity. I know that you and some other people are able to do it, but it is a true challenge for me." She was slightly embarrassed to confide this to Thomas Robert Morgan, a legendary project manager, but he obviously had a lot more insight than she did on applying PM techniques to everyday life.

Thomas chuckled. "I can see where this is a little more complicated than my plans. I just towel off and drive home in my workout clothes once rush-hour traffic has died down," he told her.

"I can do that on Thursdays when my new walking group meets," she told him, "but on Mondays and Wednesdays, I want to take a class after work at the gym and I have commitments after that."

"Let's make sure I have this clear," Thomas responded. "You have a small project; we will call it 'Ashley's Gym Project.' I don't want you to overthink this, so just answer my questions with whatever comes to your head," he guided her. "What are the tasks you need to accomplish to get this project accomplished?"

Ashley responded, "Well, I guess the first would be to have workout clothes."

Thomas wrote on a sticky note, "Prepare workout clothes."

"Does this capture your task?" he asked her, putting it on a clear section of her white board.

"Yes," she said.

"Let's break it down to the next level," Thomas Robert Morgan urged her.

"I could have a checklist and put each item in a gym bag," she said hesitantly.

"That's good," he encouraged. "Perhaps 'pack gym bag' is really the higher-level task and 'prepare workout clothes' falls under that task."

"Great." Ashley was getting enthusiastic. "I could also have a checklist with a separate toiletry kit and we could put that under 'pack gym bag' as well."

"What's the next task?" he encouraged her.

"Drive to gym," Ashley responded.

Once they had the larger tasks on the board, Thomas encouraged Ashley to look at them and distill some to the next level. She realized that making a checklist of items for her gym bag and having it ready the night before were essential. In addition, she even added that her car needed to be fueled the day prior.

Thomas continued to add sticky notes to the white board. After some additional discussion, they had over 20 sticky notes on the board and they began to organize it as a work breakdown structure, known in the project-management field as a WBS. A work breakdown structure (WBS) is a chart used to identify key tasks and break down project work into smaller, manageable chunks. It's simply a visual list of activities with no dates and no sequencing. A WBS can be high level or very detailed with multiple layers. Ashley's gym project was fairly simple, so it was possible to do with only two layers.

*A **work breakdown structure (WBS)** is a chart that represents all the work to be done in order to complete your project. It's a visual list of activities.*

"Wow," Ashley said, "this is crazy. Even for something as simple as going to the gym, there are so many tasks."

"Sometimes in training seminars I have had students create a WBS on how to bake a cake. It is amazing how many tasks our daily activities involve. You are fortunate, because you already have project-management skills. You just need to apply them to your daily life," he told her.

"You are right," she said. "My sister asked me to help her with organizing our holiday season this year and a sticky-note WBS is a great way to start. I wonder how many people are struggling with their lives because they have some of the basic concepts but aren't sure how to put them all together."

"Either that or they have the knowledge, but it doesn't occur to them that their work skills carry over into their personal lives." He added, "Ashley, you are not the first person on one of my project teams that I have had to assist with this transition. It is amazing how many people I know who can manage a multi-million-dollar budget at work but can't balance their budget at home."

This statement hit Ashley right in the gut. She knew that the next area of her life that needed to be projectized was her personal finances. She had been avoiding dealing with the aftermath of Stephen's decision to move out. The situation wasn't out of control yet, but she wasn't putting back any savings now that she had to pay for utilities and a mortgage on her own. This was something which she hated to admit but her mother warned her about.

"I need to apply some project-budgeting skills to my own life," she confessed to Thomas Robert Morgan.

"Need any assistance?" he asked gently.

"Not right now," she told him, "but I'll let you know if I run into any roadblocks. Thank you again for helping me with the gym schedule. It makes so much sense now that I see it on the board."

"No problem," Thomas responded. "I learned a long time ago that when my project team members are able to have a well-balanced life, they are better team members. After all, you can't focus completely on your job if in the back of your mind you are worried about losing your house."

That night, Ashley went home with some great ideas about how she was going to continue to use her project-management skills to improve her day-to-day life.

# THE
# BUDGET

ASHLEY HAD NOT SCHEDULED ANY social activities
for that Saturday. She knew that she had to review her
budget and she knew that would take some serious unin-
terrupted time. She set up both her laptop and her tablet
so she could have two monitors and then she started to
place the bills in piles on her dining-room table.

Ashley had met Stephen while working on a project where the homeowner wanted to integrate some unique automation features into his pool and garden. Stephen ran the landscape company that was doing the work on the project and was unlike anyone she had ever met before. He spent a lot of time outdoors and was handy around a yard and house. Ashley's dating experience had generally been with men who spent time in an office most of the day, like her father. As they say, opposites attract, and they quickly became a couple.

Despite protests from her family, she decided to purchase a house with Stephen after they had been dating for almost a year. Stephen had been enthusiastic about buying a home and having his own yard during that first year, but the novelty of homeownership had worn off and instead of becoming closer and getting married, they had grown further apart. Eventually, they were little more than roommates in the same house. Now, almost three years after they bought the house, Ashley sat at her kitchen table trying to sort through bills on her own.

She had researched household-budget apps and decided to try a free version before purchasing. From her experience in project management, she knew that there were several ways to budget for a project. One is the bottom-up method, which is what she was working on. When you have all of the known expenses, it is fairly simple to calculate the total costs of a project. In this case, her annual expenses would show her clearly what her "project budget" was from a bottom-up approach. This approach for project-management budgeting put the priority on quality over cost, as it pertained to the triple constraint of cost, time, and quality. The numbers clearly showed her what she had already known. She could not afford to continue living in the house without Stephen's income. Fortunately, the split had been amicable and Stephen was still paying his half of the mortgage until she could move out and they could sell the house.

The next approach for project-management budget estimating that she wanted to apply was the top-down method of budgeting. When a project manager knows that they have a fixed budget, they use that figure to determine what they could purchase within their budget, placing the greatest emphasis on cost as it pertains to the triple constraint. With her budget estimate and some research on townhomes in the Washington Park neighborhood, she was reasonably certain that purchasing a townhome closer to the Denver Technical Center (DTC) would be within her budget. Her yard would be a lot smaller and a lot easier to maintain. Without Stephen there to landscape, it was not being maintained the way it should be for all the features he had installed. Another benefit would be that she would be closer to work and save on both commuting time and gas. She would also be closer to downtown for social activities and have access to the light rail. Most importantly, she would be able to spend more time with Cupcake and take him to downtown activities, unlike in the suburbs.

One of the commonly used project-management budgeting techniques is analogous estimating. This technique is used when a PM has access to a similar project and can use that data. In this case, there was plenty of information available on the internet for average utility costs in the neighborhood for Ashley to develop an estimate that fit her top-down budget.

After spending several hours getting her budget organized, Ashley felt like she had a solid idea of what was possible both within the Denver housing market and her fiscal constraints. She knew what she needed to do. She realized that just addressing and identifying her budget problems had helped her to feel better. Cupcake, on the other hand, didn't care about her budget. He was pacing between her and the door and she knew she had best take him for his evening walk. As she walked around the neighborhood, she understood it was time to take control of her life as a project and to start getting serious about moving.

# Not the Only Convert

**THE NEXT WEEK AT WORK** was busier than usual and the new building was starting to take shape. Ashley met with Troy from Construction and some of his direct reports on the HVAC system being installed. The project goal was to have the HVAC system completely integrated into the smart grid. Meeting early and communicating often as the construction work took place allowed Ashley to seamlessly integrate the system.

"I appreciate you and your team including me on all aspects of your construction as it occurs," she told Troy. "I have been on projects where I didn't find out changes until well afterward or no one remembered to tell me at all," she admitted.

"Thomas Robert Morgan is serious about communications on his projects." He smiled. "I have been with him a few years and it took me the first couple of projects to learn what he meant by overcommunicating." He chuckled. "The first few projects, he was on me all the time to share more. I was already sharing more than I had ever done before, but it was never enough. Now I understand why, but in those early days, it was a significant challenge."

"In my role as IT integration, I feel like I normally have to beg for information. This is honestly the best large team that I have ever worked with," Ashley said with a smile. "Even the construction lead is nice."

"Working with the boss will change you," Troy said. "The first email I got from him, I remember thinking that his tagline on his signature block was a typical marketing phrase. I had no idea back then that I would become a convert to 'Life is a Project,'" he confessed.

"Really?" Ashley asked. "I am working through how to apply more project management into my daily life."

"I'm not surprised," Troy told her. "When I first

started working for Thomas, he told me that if I didn't start managing my life like a project, I was doomed for failure. I'm a big construction guy. My first thought was that I didn't care that this guy played as a wide receiver for Alabama, he couldn't talk to me like that."

Ashley was shocked. "Mr. Morgan really called you a failure?"

"He didn't call me a failure, but he pointed out that my life was headed in that direction. I had a lot of personal issues going on back in those days and they were always impacting my work. I would show up late a lot and was distracted by my personal problems at work. When the boss started working with me on 'projectizing' my lifestyle, I didn't buy into it much."

"I think that the first time he mentioned it to me, I felt like he could read my mind. It never occurred to me to apply my PM skills to my personal life." Ashley felt so good to be sharing the project-management lifestyle with another team member.

"I wish I hadn't been so hardheaded," Troy admitted. "Once I stopped resisting and started actually applying project-management techniques to my lifestyle, I saw improvements right away."

"Thank you for sharing with me," Ashley gushed to Troy. "It is so wonderful to be able to talk to someone who has already projectized their lifestyle."

"Keep applying it one step at a time, just like any other project," he told her. "No project is perfect and no life is perfect, but we can keep striving to improve both."

"Thanks," Ashley told him. "My next step is going to be creating a mini-project plan to move to a new house."

"Wow," Troy said, "you must be embracing the project-management lifestyle in every way. Keep working at it and feel free to ask anyone who has worked with Thomas Robert Morgan for help."

"You are all converts?" Ashley asked.

"I'll ask you what you think when we are closing this project," Troy told her with a smile. "Also, if you need help with the move, let me know. I spend way too much time in offices these days and am more than happy to carry a few boxes."

"Thanks," Ashley replied. "I might have to take you up on it."

# THE PROJECT LIFECYCLE – MOVING

**ASHLEY WAS EMBRACING HOW TO** apply her project-management skills on a small scale to plan her move. The project-management lifecycle consists of five phases: initiating, planning, executing, monitoring and controlling, and closing. She had already begun the initiating phase of the project, but she wanted to go through each phase in detail to test her new skills at projectizing her lifestyle.

She wouldn't need to use all of the elements of project management, like they did for the smart building, but basic project management would make the move a lot smoother.

*The **project lifecycle** consists of five phases: initiating, planning, executing, monitoring and controlling, and closing. Each phase has process groups that are associated. There will rarely be a case in your personal projects in which you have to use all of the process groups.*

Every project has five phases. The initiating phase of a project is when the project scope is clearly defined and a project charter is created. The planning phase of a project is the aspect of project management where details are planned and this is where tools like budgeting, work breakdown structures, Gantt charts, and other project-management tools are developed. The execution phase is when the plans get applied and the work gets accomplished. The controlling and monitoring phase happens during the execution and this is when the project manager ensures everything stays on track. The final phase of any project is the closing phase.

Ashley realized that in previous moves, some basic project management could have prevented a lot of the problems that she experienced. The first person she consulted was of course her project manager and mentor, Thomas Robert Morgan.

"Great idea," he told her. "I think that every move is a small project and that using your PM skills will help you to plan your move. Please let me know anything I can do to assist."

"I know I have the foundational skills to plan a successful move project, but I will be sure to ask you any questions as they come up," she told him, excited about this new project in her life. She knew that moving into a more cost-effective place and a new neighborhood would be beneficial to balancing the triple constraint of cost, time, and value in her daily life.

## Initiating Phase

She decided to jump straight into the project initiating phase. The initiating phase of a project is when the project charter is created. A project charter is the defining document for a project and captures the essence of a project. The project objectives, obstacles, pros and cons, stakeholders, projected cost, final date, and constraints are captured in this document. In this case, she could skip quite a few steps, because she was the project manager and the project champion. The project champion is generally somebody at a higher level in the organization who synchronizes the project and ensures stakeholder buy-in. In her previous jobs doing IT project management, most often the CIO was the project champion.

She wanted to take the time to fully capture the constraints of her project. She had a limited budget and she needed to ensure that she didn't get a new place that was too large or that wouldn't meet her needs. In addition, she needed to identify the obstacles to selling her current home. Despite her initial optimism, Ashley realized that her move was a much larger project than she had first thought. She decided that she needed to write down her scope and document it in a template document, so she needed a project charter after all.

The initiating phase of a project only has two process groups: creating the charter, which she had finally finished, and identifying the stakeholders. The two primary stakeholders were of course Ashley and Cupcake, but he couldn't talk, so it made things easier. She would be consulting with her mother and sister for input and feedback, but ultimately, this was her project.

After a weekend of initiating her move, Ashley was ready to get back to work. She knew that scoping her social activities and creating a WBS for the gym ensured that her week went by smoothly. Maybe she would even have time to start working on the planning phase during the week. Instead of feeling stressed and making a mental list of all the things she needed to do, for the first time that she could remember, she fell asleep quickly on a Sunday night.

The next day while Ashley was working at her old company office, Chris stopped by, hanging out in her doorway. "Can I say something without offending you?" he asked.

Ashley looked up, surprised. Chris wasn't known for filtering his thoughts, so this should be interesting. "Sure," she said encouragingly.

"I just wanted to say that I can tell you have been working out the past few weeks and you look great." He smiled, his dimples showing. "I just wanted to tell you to encourage you, but not to creep you out."

"Creeping women out, isn't that your trademark?" Mark said, coming up behind him. "Seriously, Ashley, whatever you are doing, keep it up. You are looking more relaxed than I have seen you in years and the feedback that we are getting from the smart-building project is terrific. There is even some talk of potential follow-on work," Mark added proudly.

"Thanks, guys." Ashley smiled at her colleagues. "I have been working on this 'Life is a Project' concept from Mr. Morgan and it is changing my whole life. I even reviewed my budget and decided that I need to move to someplace closer to work and more affordable."

"Guess that means you'll expect us to help move boxes when the time comes," Chris replied.

"I think that is great," Mark told her. "I know that once the girls move out, Martha and I are thinking about downsizing. We will have to review our finances and other plans, just like you are now," he added. "Speaking of which, what exactly are these changes which Mr. Morgan has you implementing in your personal life?"

"You know how whenever you get an email from Mr. Morgan that his signature block reads, 'Life is a Project'? Well, he truly believes that and lives by it," she told her coworkers.

"That is kind of interesting," Chris said. "Maybe if you are going to be in the office one day this week, the three of us could have lunch in the conference room and talk about it some more. Everyone knows that Robert Thomas Morgan is a true leader in project management."

Mark slapped Chris on the back. "I hate to admit when you are right, but that is a great idea. Let's talk more about 'Life is a Project' the next time you are in our office, Ashley. As you know, I am a big fan of work–life balance and this sounds like an interesting way to achieve that." Then he added, "Right now, I need to get back to my own projects."

As Mark and Chris walked away, Ashley realized that "Life is a Project" was an idea worth sharing. She also decided to set up the calendar invite right then for lunch with her coworkers to discuss projectizing their lives. She wanted to share her experiences with them. She knew for sure that Mark would embrace the concept.

The week flew by and she had a great lunch with Mark and Chris about "Life is a Project." Mark understood the concept immediately and they discussed how he could apply it to his work–life balance approach. Chris wasn't as interested at first, but realized that he needed to start writing out his goals. He talked a lot about getting an executive MBA, but had done nothing more than just read about programs on the internet. Ashley shared her gym WBS concept and move plan with her colleagues. By the end of lunch, all three had some new ideas on how they would projectize their lives.

That weekend, she would move from the initiating to the planning phase.

## Planning Phase

Ashley set aside most of the weekend to work on the planning phase of her personal move project. The first process group that she needed to tackle was the project scope. The triple constraint of her project would of course be based on the cost, time, and value she applied to this move. Her initial budget estimates were great to address the cost and resources she would need. She realized that she would need to take time away from the office for at least a few days for the move and that she would need to adjust this around the project schedule for the smart building.

As she worked through the details of the process groups in the planning phase, she decided that she should consult with one of her teammates on the smart-building project.

One of the things that she was finding the most enjoyable about the smart-building project was interacting with the members of the project team. The person that she wanted to speak with about scoping the project was Jim Brown, the architect for their project. He had been on board since before she was, and part of the team prior to the project charter.

"How's it going, Jim?" she asked, pausing at his office door.

"Great." Jim smiled from his desk. "Come on in," he invited her. Jim's office was full of rolled-up architectural designs and open designs spread all over every flat surface. He assisted Ashley with moving some of the papers so she could take a seat. "Sorry about the mess," he said, gesturing around his office. "Occupational hazard."

"No worries," Ashley replied. "My office can get pretty crazy, too. I wanted to talk to you about the design at the beginning of the project," she told him.

"Are you worried about the design and the IT integration?" he asked with concern.

"No," Ashley responded. "The design is great and so far, the entire project team has been great about letting me know when there are changes and how they impact my work. Like you, this is my first time working with Thomas Robert Morgan, and I was wondering how the design and scope were captured for the project. It just seems that this project team does a better job of actually following all of the project-management standards than teams at other projects I have been on," she added.

"I have to admit that I am embracing being a part of this project and now I understand your question. This certainly is a different project team to work around. The entire team seems to buy into the need to overcommunicate. When we agreed on the design, Thomas Robert Morgan was very strict on capturing everything and freezing it at that moment. I have never seen a project manager so adamant. He told everyone in the room that the scope was now set and that changes needed to go through a complete change-review process."

"That certainly sounds like Mr. Morgan," Ashley said. "How many changes have there been to the design since we started three months ago?"

"We actually have had very few changes," he told her. "There have been some changes to interior walls, a few doorways and entrances, but nothing like I have seen in the past with other projects."

Jim provided some additional details regarding the change-management process and how these changes were accepted or denied.

"Thanks for sharing this with me," Ashley told Jim. "I appreciate your time and you and your team keeping me informed of even the minor changes."

"Anytime," Jim said. "This might be the first project team that I have ever been on where I don't cringe every time one of the team members from another division comes by. Sort of sad, when you think about how many bad projects I've been on," he reflected.

"I think it is having a great project manager who truly lives by the standards," Ashley responded over her shoulder as she left the office.

Jim smiled. "I have never met a project manager like Thomas Robert Morgan before. He honestly believes that everything is a project."

Then they both quoted, "Life is a Project" at the same time and started laughing.

As Ashley walked down the hall, she realized that both her work projects and her personal projects would benefit from more demanding scoping and then only being changed after going through change management. Scope creep—when requirements just keep getting added and often without proper documentation—was a major issue in her previous projects. Especially in the ones where trust-fund kids just kept making demands, but they didn't understand the real cost that their changes required.

She was fairly disciplined when it came to work, but she had never before applied this to her personal life. She had constantly adjusted her budget and schedule, not fully considering the value of the activities she engaged in. She was determined to do a better job on this in the future.

Now that she had a better understanding of how Thomas Robert Morgan had been so successful, she felt inspired to continue both at work and at home. She had been a little skeptical at first when Mr. Morgan had explained his theory that life was a project, but now that she was seeing results, she wanted to continue. She didn't have much time during the week, but she spent at least half an hour each evening on her personal project plan. She knew from work that it was better to take extra time on the planning phase and not rush into execution.

Ashley reviewed her time-management process group again. She had decided that she would list her current home while still looking for a new house. She knew that if her home sold before she was able to find and close on a new townhouse in the neighborhood she wanted, then she might have to stay in a temporary apartment and possibly put her belongings in storage, but this was an acceptable risk. She captured the risk and annotated it in her risk-management plan.

It took her almost a month, but she completed her project plan and had addressed each of the twelve process areas of project planning, at least on a high level. This included integration management, scope management, time management, cost management, quality management, human resource management, communications management, risk management, and procurement management. She had been surprised to realize how each of the twelve process groups actually applied to a project as small as her personal move. She realized that without going through the process groups, she would have left out some key elements.

As Ashley developed her plan, she consulted often with Troy, the construction manager. He was a great resource to bounce ideas off of and gave her some practical advice based on his experiences. She got into the habit of stopping by Troy's office for coffee a few days a week. While she was talking to Troy in his office, Terri Lewis in Human Resources joined them sometimes and gave her perspective.

Terri was a longtime convert to projectizing her life and enjoyed sharing her input with others. She was the only member of the team who had worked for Thomas Robert Morgan longer than Troy.

Now that her plan was written, she knew it was time to execute. She wanted to ensure that the next phase— execution—would be completed before the Denver winter set upon the city. She had developed several easy checklists to aid her in this process. She would need to contact a real-estate agent first. She was ready to move to the execution phase of her small project. Ashley loved the planning phase of a project, the phase where the project manager has control. She always found the execution phase a little scary; this is the phase when reality derails the best plans. In the past, Ashley had not been rigorous in planning her personal life. She had some peace of mind this time; this was the most detailed plan she had ever completed for her personal life.

## Execution Phase

The execution phase of her project began with a meeting with a real-estate agent. She decided to go with someone who was recommended by Jim Brown, the architect on the smart building. She needed someone who would understand her requirements both for selling her current home and for buying her new home near Washington Park. Ellen, her new agent, scheduled the photos and other details for her current home.

When Ellen came by the house, she was immediately impressed with the landscaping. "This looks just like the work of Stephen Jones," she gushed.

"He designed it all," Ashley told her. "It is an integrated smart-technology system that supports the irrigation system, water features, solar panels, and the patio shaders."

"This will be featured in the listing," Ellen told her. "Why didn't you tell me about this before?"

Ashley smiled a little sadly. "I guess after you live with Stephen Jones's work for so long, you just aren't as impressed anymore."

"Well, you certainly have a house ready to sell," Ellen exclaimed. "I know this will go quickly once it is listed, so we need to start looking at those townhouses as soon as you can."

Ashley fell in love with the first townhouse that she looked at. Ellen took her to several more, but she knew that the first one was destined to be her new home. She quickly made a bid and after a quick counteroffer with the condition of almost two months until closing, everything was agreed upon. Ellen spoke to the seller's agent and found out that the owner was moving out of state and didn't want to move into a temporary place. Ashley agreed to the terms, deciding that cost was more important than the schedule, in this case. She also reasoned that this would give her current house time to sell.

As the days passed, there were several viewings of her current home but no offers. Ashley reviewed her risk registry and tried to relax, reminding herself that she had plans in case the house didn't sell right away. She went through her checklists and packed her belongings to prepare for the move. Because she was downsizing, there was also a lot that she needed to sell or donate to charity. Her mom, Brittany, and the kids came by a few times to help with the packing.

On move-in day, everything went surprisingly well. Chris, Mark, and Troy all showed up to help move boxes, and so did her brother-in-law Jake and a few of the guys from her gym. Her mother wielded one of her checklists at the house she was moving out of and Brittany waited at the townhouse with another. The move went more smoothly than she had imagined and by the end of the day, everyone was eating pizza and sharing stories on her patio—the only area at her new townhouse where the furniture wasn't covered in boxes.

Right after she bit into a slice of pepperoni, her cell phone rang.

"You have an offer on your house," Ellen informed her. "The potential buyers love your backyard and Stephen's work. They are willing to give you your asking price."

"That's great," Ashley responded, surprised. After all of these weeks with no offer, to get her asking price was a gigantic shock.

"I know you just moved today," Ellen said. "I will send you the paperwork and you can sign everything from your smart phone."

Ashley could feel everyone looking at her. "I just got an offer for my asking price for my old house in the suburbs," she told them.

Everyone clapped and told her "Congratulations." This was the best news she could have gotten. The physical move had gone smoothly and now she would be able to sell her old house. The hard work now would be unpacking all of the boxes.

That night, Ashley reviewed her personal project plan and the five process groups for execution. She reflected on how each process had been executed well that day. The direction and management process group had executed perfectly. Her mom and sister had been invaluable to her with the quality management at both the old and new house. Her human-resource team had been great and worked for pizza. Her communications had improved greatly and she had created a group chat space, which made it easy for everyone to share information. The truck had been picked up and returned on time to the agency, so she even was able to check off the procurement process group.

She was glad that she had separated out her bed linens and pillows; it was very nice to be able to sleep in her bed in her new townhouse. All in all, it was the best move ever, she decided as she went to sleep with Cupcake at her feet.

## Monitoring and Controlling Phase

Moving didn't stop work and on Monday Ashley was back in her office at the smart building. She spent her day focused on reports. When she was reviewing one of the bills from one of her subcontractors, she realized there was a discrepancy and made a note. She called Carl Nelson's office and left a message for him that they needed to talk first thing in the morning. *Always best to ask the lawyer*, she thought to herself.

The next morning, Carl stopped by Ashley's desk while she was drinking her morning coffee.

"Good morning, Ashley," he said, carrying his own cup of coffee. "I read the documents you emailed me from your subcontractor. I see the same issues you do.

Let's try calling them together to see if this is just a billing mistake and if they don't agree to correct it, there are other legal actions we can take."

"I've worked with them before," she told Carl. "I honestly think this is just an accounting error or a typo, but I didn't want to take any action before you reviewed it. That is why we pay you lawyers so much money," she added with a laugh. Carl was one of the most down-to-earth lawyers she had ever met. Of course you had to be to work on Thomas Robert Morgan's project team.

Together Ashley and Carl called her subcontractor and they were able to quickly resolve the issue. The subcontractor promised to send a new invoice right away and apologized profusely for the error.

"Well, that went well," Ashley said after they were off the call. "I'm so glad because this vendor is terrific and I would like to use them again."

"It was a simple error and one that could have gone unnoticed," Carl pointed out. "I am glad this project team has great people who take their jobs seriously. It is a lot easier to fix errors in the monitoring and controlling phase, before we pay the bills. It is a lot harder to try to recoup money when an auditor finds an error during project closing."

"Thanks," Ashley replied. "I was just doing my

normal reports and noticed the error. I'm glad that it turned out to be minor. No offense, but the last thing I need is a bunch of lawyers involved."

"No offense taken." Carl laughed. "I have heard plenty of lawyer jokes in my time. By the way, Thomas Robert Morgan mentioned that he has been working with you on projectizing your lifestyle. How is it going?"

"Even better than I could have imagined when Mr. Morgan told me about his concept," Ashley told him, surprised the lawyer knew. "I actually just moved into my new townhouse and developing a project plan helped the move to go smoothly and reduced stress for everyone involved."

"When Thomas Robert Morgan started to lecture me on how project management could help my life, I thought he was crazy. After all, I'm a lawyer; we know how to handle everything in life—just ask us," he said with a chuckle. "Now, after working with Thomas Robert Morgan for several years, I can't imagine my life without basic PM tools."

"Really?" Ashley was surprised by both Carl's openness and his vulnerability. "You needed project management in your life?"

"I used to be all work all the time," he told her. "I would only get a few hours of sleep every night and then be right back in the office checking email, reading depositions—it was crazy. Mr. Morgan came to me one day and told me I was going to work myself into an early grave. He told me that I needed to scope my life around my values. It was completely different than anything I had ever heard in law school, but I also knew that I was burning myself out."

"So even though you aren't a project manager, you still embraced projectizing your lifestyle?" She encouraged him to go on.

"It wasn't that hard once I started. Mr. Morgan helped me to find some simple templates online when I needed them and was always there for advice and encouragement." He paused and added, "I think sometimes it might be harder for those with PM backgrounds. I didn't know anything about project management and just use simple techniques and tools for daily life. I think sometimes those of you with PM backgrounds try to overcomplicate things."

"Thanks for the advice," Ashley told him. "Both for the help with my vendor and life as a project. I'll keep you informed on how it goes."

"I'll look forward to your updates and let me know if you need any help with your move," he added.

"All the boxes were moved this weekend," she told him. "Now I just have to sort them all out. I don't even know where half my things are yet."

"Just take it slow," Carl advised, "and seriously, if there is anything I can help with, let me know. We are actually a team here, in every way."

After Carl left her office, Ashley reflected on how, with projects at the office, just like in life, the monitoring and controlling phase happen during execution. She was glad that she had noticed the accounting error and that the vendor had been so agreeable. She knew that when she got home that evening, she'd need to give the same due diligence to her move project.

She also followed Carl's advice and sent an email over to Jason Lee in Contracting to let him know about the error that they had uncovered and the discussion with the vendor. It was great that everything had worked out, but she wanted Jason to have a copy in his records.

In the case of Ashley's relocation project, she was most concerned with the schedule and the cost controls. She wanted to be very aggressive on closing on her old house, because the bills were already coming in on her new townhouse.

She had built some slack into her timeline in case the old house didn't sell, but now that she had an offer, she didn't want to wait. She had already cut into her savings and once the old house sold, she would be able to replenish most of her savings. With a lower mortgage payment and utilities, she would also be able to start putting back savings each month again. Saving money for retirement and a new emergency fund was of course outside of the current project.

Ashley reviewed the process groups that were conducted in the monitoring and controlling phase. She felt that both the overall project and scope were still on track. She had a few concerns with schedule and costs, but she had already addressed those and her risks. She took a quick look at her checklists for quality control, communications, and procurements to make sure that there were no outstanding issues with those.

"Come on, Cupcake," Ashley called out to the dog. "Let's go for a walk. Our life's project seems to be back on track." As Ashley walked Cupcake around her new neighborhood, she thought about the changes in her life that had occurred since starting to work for Thomas Robert Morgan. The things she was doing were simple but so effective. For the first time in a long time, she felt optimistic about her future.

## Closing Phase

As Ashley sat at the title company signing the mortgage papers across from the happy couple purchasing her home, the moment was bittersweet. A few years ago, she had been part of a happy couple purchasing a home and now she was on the other side of the table.

Stephen wasn't able to make it and had already signed all of the documents which required his signature. In life, she reflected, you needed to be prepared for change management and to rescope your life when required. She loved her new townhouse and neighborhood. As she signed the last of the documents, she knew she was making the right choice for her own life's project.

"We promise, we'll take great care of the backyard," the happy wife told Ashley as she handed over her last set of keys. Ashley waved goodbye as the couple walked out of the room.

As soon as Ashley arrived at her new townhouse, she realized that she needed to conduct a complete project closeout. She had a checklist that included all of the utilities that she needed to cancel at her old house. No point in paying utilities and other bills for a house which she no longer owned. This part of the project closeout made her feel a bit better.

Like the initiating phase, the closing phase also has only two process groups: closing the project and closing procurements. The closing phase, even though one of the shortest, was often overlooked and completed incorrectly. Often team members were rushing to their next project instead of taking the time to properly close their current project. Ashley wanted to capture all of her lessons learned and write a blog post about it to share on a site she had used to prepare for her move; maybe it would help people in their future moves.

*Sometimes even work projects can be emotionally hard to close*, she thought. When they were finished with the smart building, many of the team members would go their separate ways, to include her mentor, Thomas Robert Morgan. They were barely over halfway through the project, but the thought of the project closing wasn't a happy one. So much had changed for Ashley in such a short amount of time. She still felt that she had so much more to learn, though, and time would go by so quickly.

# SCOPING
# THE HOLIDAYS

**ASHLEY HAD SET A REMINDER** on her phone back in late summer to talk to her family about their holiday plans. She was surprised when her phone reminder pinged. Wow, was it already the week before Halloween? Her life had only just gotten a little less chaotic and she knew the holidays could undo all of her work toward a more organized lifestyle.

Ashley scheduled a time to meet with her mother and her sister. Every year, the time between Halloween and New Year's Eve was chaotic. The three women discussed how they could use some of Ashley's project-management techniques for daily life and apply these techniques to the holidays.

"We have to scope our holidays," Ashley said. She explained the concept of the triple constraint of cost, schedule, and value and how this could be applied to the holidays. "Every year we are in debt, stressed, and exhausted after the holidays," she concluded. "That shows a complete lack of balance in our holidays as a project."

"So," her sister Brittany responded, "you think that if we decide on a scope for our holidays, we will be better off?" She didn't sound confident in the idea.

"One of the techniques in project management to ensure that requirements are captured is conducting a facilitated workshop." She paused, thinking the process through. "Let's ask each member of the family their top five activities that we do for the holidays. This will capture the requirements."

"This has to include Jared, Jessica, and my husband Jake," Brittany said.

"Of course," Ashley replied. "They are stakeholders, too."

"Stakeholders?" her mom asked.

"A project-management term for people who have a stake in the project," Ashley told her. "For this project, each of the stakeholders will write down their top five activities. Then we can determine the resources and time that each requirement uses. We will ask everyone to prioritize their top five activities so that we know the value."

"Well," her mother Gloria said, "I don't see how this can hurt."

Gloria found some paper and they took it into the living room where the other three were watching a movie. They explained the idea of coming up with the top five holiday activities and helped the children write down their lists.

Once they had all the lists, they created a consolidated master list.

"Wow," Brittany observed, "there are some activities that we do every year that didn't make anyone's list. Neither of the kids put down seeing Santa as an activity."

"Yes," Gloria said. "Also, in some cases, multiple people put down the same activity. I'm glad one is creating food baskets at Christmas for the homeless shelter."

"At least we know what is important to every family member," Ashley said. "Now we can allocate our resources, both time and money, to the things that truly add value to our holidays."

"Think about the time and stress we can save by not doing activities that aren't even important," Brittany said. "Ashley," she added, "this might be the best plan you have had, Little Sister."

"Thanks." Ashley beamed with the praise. She also started to think about how many other families were overwhelmed because they tried to do too much during the holidays. Could project management help other families reduce their stress?

After about an hour, they felt satisfied that this year, the holidays would be focused on activities that really mattered while costing less and being less hectic from doing too many activities. Both Jessica and Jared would get to participate in their top three activities and most of the things that didn't make anybody's activity list would be cut.

# Recognizing the Need for Risk Management

**THE NEXT WEEKEND, ASHLEY DISCOVERED** another aspect of project management that could be applied to her daily life. Her discovery came unexpectedly during lunch. She had prepared a turkey sandwich with light mayo when she heard the doorbell ring. Leaving her just-completed sandwich on the table, she went to find out who was at the door.

After quickly explaining to a pushy salesman that she had no interest in switching to a new cable-service provider, as she hadn't even received a bill yet for her current service, she returned to the kitchen. There stood Cupcake, his front paws on the kitchen table, enjoying her turkey sandwich. Part of Ashley wanted to snap a quick picture to share on her social-media accounts, but she did not want to encourage bad behavior. She scolded Cupcake and sent him to his own food dish in the corner. Then she tossed the half-eaten-by-doggie sandwich and started over.

While working on the second sandwich, she started to think about project-risk management. Not planning for risk as it pertained to a simple turkey sandwich wasn't a significant issue, but what about risk regarding her new budget? Any time that you have to buy a new home and sell one, there are a lot of risks.

She could almost hear Thomas Robert Morgan's voice in her head. *What would you do for a project at work?*

"Conduct a risk analysis," she answered the voice in her head.

What other areas in her life needed risk management? Since Stephen had left, she had avoided dating anyone, because of the risk. She and her sister had become very protective of her mother since their father passed away. There was certainly plenty of opportunity for risk management in regards to her surviving parent. She also knew that there was a lot of risk as a single person and being the sole provider for all of her bills. Ashley realized that there were several areas in her life that would benefit from risk management and the best way to do this was to create a risk register.

*Risk management is the identification, assessment, and prioritization of risks followed by coordinated application of resources to minimize, monitor, and control the probability and/or impact of events or to maximize the realization of opportunities.*

Ashley started to create a simple risk register on her laptop from a template to quickly capture all of the thoughts in her head. She created columns for category, name, probability, impact, mitigation, contingency, and the total score.

Some of the areas that she felt she needed to focus on in life were financial. She and her sister had been discussing the unexpected death of their father and how this had impacted their lives. She desperately needed to review her insurance policies to include life, long-term care, and health. She also needed to look at those same policies for her mother.

For some of the risks involving her mother, she realized that she would need to consult with her mom and sister. After a few hours, she felt satisfied with her draft risk register. It was time to put everything away and take Cupcake for a walk in the park. Not walking the dog on time had its own risks, she told herself.

The next time she was in the office, she and Troy were discussing how risk management could be applied to daily life when Carl entered her office.

"I came by to let you know that I reviewed the new contract for the cloud vendor," Carl told her. "Jason is out of the office today and I didn't want you to have to wait for the news."

"Great," Ashley responded with a smile. "Troy and I were just discussing risk management, and getting this vendor approved to start working and not holding up the project schedule was starting to trigger some of my risk-management criteria."

"Well, I'm always glad to come in and save the day," Carl joked. "It's not often that lawyers are seen as the good guys. Are there other areas of the project that you are concerned about risk in right now?" Carl asked.

"Not this project," Ashley said, "but my life as a project."

"I am trying to give Ashley some advice from my lessons learned over the past few years," Troy told him. "That should be enough for a book," Carl responded good-naturedly.

"That's for sure," Troy said. "I thought Thomas Robert Morgan was going to take me out to some old football field and make me do drills until I could figure out how to apply some risk management to my own life."

The three discussed risk management in daily life for a few more minutes and then had to get back to their work project. Ashley was excited that she could move forward with the cloud-vendor contract. This was a task that had a lot of risk because it was on her critical path. The critical path of a project comprises the activities required to complete the project on schedule.

This made Ashley wonder what tasks should be on her own life's critical path. She knew this was an important idea, but it would have to wait until after the holidays.

# Holiday
# Planning Beyond
# the Family

**As Ashley drove to work,** she listened to the 24-hour Christmas radio station. She felt confident with the priorities she had developed with her family to projectize the holidays. She could already tell that both her mother and sister were less stressed and more cheerful. Thanksgiving was over and the other holidays were quickly approaching.

One area that was still bothering her was all of the Christmas cards she needed to send and people that she needed to call. In addition, she had received several invitations to parties and events that didn't involve her immediate family.

When she went to her office, she selected a Christmas playlist and started to go through her emails. After completing her morning email reading, she began making phone calls to the leads for her vendors and subcontractors that she needed to contact to complete action items and get project-status updates. Before she knew it, her alarm chimed at her desk to remind her to meet with Terri Lewis in Human Resources.

"Hey, Terri," Ashley said, meeting Terri in the entryway to the building. "Ready for lunch?" Terri and Ashley had started going to lunch together every Wednesday to get away from the office and try some of the different local lunch options.

"You look like you are bundled up against the Denver winter cold." Terri smiled, pulling her own scarf a little tighter. The two women walked swiftly to a small deli around the corner. They ordered soup and sandwiches and then headed to a table.

"How is your week going?" Ashley asked.

"Things are getting overwhelmingly busy in my department," Terri told her. "We are on schedule for the project to be completed in March and that means I have to start working to close out this project and start planning for the next."

"It is hard to believe that we are three-quarters of the way through the project," Ashley told her. "It seems like just last week when we had the kickoff meeting."

"We have certainly done a lot in a short time," Terri said. "It has been great to see you progress through the process of projectizing your life," she told her with a smile. "It is always great to watch as people go through their journey. I have worked with Mr. Morgan for a long time and I have seen a lot of people that he has influenced with his philosophy. You are certainly someone who has applied the techniques quickly."

"Thanks, Terri," Ashley responded. "It has also been great to get to know someone who has successfully applied project management to their lives."

"It's not always easy," Terri confessed, "but it is certainly worth it. I seriously struggled for the first few years with the holidays and project management."

"As you know, I am tackling it this year for the first time," Ashley said. "I met with my mom and sister and we did some early planning, but I hadn't completely considered all of the activities and communications outside of my family."

"What aspects are you struggling with?" Terri asked.

"As someone who has never been a project manager, I found that the holidays were true challenges for me. Thomas Robert Morgan suggested that I do a RACI chart for my annual holiday party."

A **RACI chart** is a matrix of all the activities or decision-making authorities undertaken in an organization, set against all the people or roles. At each intersection of activity and role, it is possible to assign somebody responsible, accountable, consulted, or informed for that activity or decision.

"Really?" Ashley was surprised. A RACI chart is a matrix that shows the roles and responsibilities for activities in a project. "How exactly did he apply it?" she asked.

"Once I understood it, it was fairly simple," Terri said, drawing a RACI chart on the back of a napkin. "For each holiday activity, you assign a role. Who is responsible? Who is accountable? Who is consulted? And who is informed? For example, if you are hosting a Christmas party, you are the one responsible. A caterer might be accountable for the food. A DJ might be accountable for music. All sorts of people might be consulted on ideas. Your entire guest list is informed."

"That is a great idea," Ashley said. "A RACI chart could be used for any larger party or activity. I used one for my recent move. But what about when you aren't hosting the party or other activities?"

"For that, Thomas suggested a communication management plan," Terri told her.

"That makes a lot of sense," Ashley reflected. "I just spent my morning going through emails, making phone calls, and setting tasks for follow-up. Every week, we have to send out a detailed project update report to Thomas so that he can have the big picture of the entire project. I could set up a small plan like that for the holidays."

"That is what I do," Terri told her. "It is like doing a Christmas-card list on crack!"

As they braved the Denver cold and walked back to the office, Ashley felt more in control of her life than she had in a long time. Even the holidays had not derailed her.

She went home that night and created a communication management plan for the holidays. People she wanted to send cards out to, people she wanted to get small presents for, parties she wanted to attend, and people with whom she wanted to catch up and have a cup of coffee. She also tracked whether she would contact people by social media, email, phone calls, or in person. Using project management and applying it to her daily life was becoming routine. She wondered who else could benefit from some basic project management in their daily lives.

# THE
# CRITICAL PATH

---

**IT WAS NEW YEAR'S DAY.** Ashley normally wrote a lot of resolutions, which she knew she would never keep. One of the resolutions on her list every year was to start going to the gym and lose weight. This year she had created a work breakdown structure in August, with Thomas Robert Morgan, as one of her first steps in her attempt to apply project management to her daily life.

Now, going to the gym and being a part of a walking group were part of her routine. She and some friends were even planning to run a 5k race in the spring. Realizing how project management had made such a positive impact in her life, she wanted to do something different this year.

Ashley reflected on critical-path analysis and how it could be applied to a life. In her first conversation with Thomas Robert Morgan, he pointed out that every life, like every project, had a beginning and an end. Her critical path needed to include the activities in her life that she wanted to leave behind as a legacy. She reasoned that she may not know when her life would end. After all, her entire family was unprepared for her father's heart attack. Instead, she needed to create a critical path of the important things that she wanted to accomplish and build each day of her life toward those things. Going to the gym was important, because being fit and healthy would allow her to accomplish more.

She brought out her list of priorities from the early summer, when she first began this journey.

- ☐ Family (to include Cupcake)
- ☐ Relationships (friends and social acquaintances)
- ☐ Self-development
- ☐ Charity work
- ☐ Health and fitness

She was on track with some, but not all. One of the activities that stood out was self-development. Now that she had her finances and schedule under control, it was time to start getting serious about earning a master's degree. It was something she talked about often, but knew she should put it on her critical path.

Another area that she needed to consider was charity work. She and her family volunteered to donate food baskets every year, but she wanted to do more. God had given her so many opportunities and she had a pretty amazing life. How could she give back? One of her friends had told her about a program helping middle-school girls train for a 5K run. She was already going to do this with her friends, so why not assist a girl in need? She decided to immediately email her friend Sonya to find out more about the program.

She wrote down a few more things she wanted to accomplish, like starting college funds for her niece and nephew. She would be able to add more to these every year.

Ashley built a critical path showing the activities that she wanted to achieve in the next year. She sincerely hoped that this would not be the end of her life as a project. She knew that instead of New Year's resolutions, she would be monitoring her critical path in the future.

# CHANGE
# MANAGEMENT

---

**AT THE END OF THE** next project meeting, Thomas Robert Morgan asked, "Ashley, do you mind coming by my office before you leave today?"

"Of course, sir," she responded. "What time is good for you?"

"About four thirty would be great," he said and turned to leave.

Ashley was curious about what he wanted, but knew it would have to wait for the end of the day. She spent the afternoon focused on some change requests that were being processed for the project. Most of the changes were minor and wouldn't have any significant impact on the triple constraint. Ashley could almost hear Mr. Morgan's voice in her head reminding the team to always ensure that changes did not have a significant impact to the cost, schedule, or product quality. She was surprised when her computer calendar alarm chimed, reminding her that she needed to head over to Mr. Morgan's office.

"Ashley"—he smiled at her—"please come in and have a seat." While Ashley was getting settled into the chair indicated, he said, "So, I hear that you have been applying your project-management skills to your life and even based your entire move around it."

"Yes, I did," she told him. "I know that this helped my move to be more organized and go more smoothly."

"I just wanted to remind you that I am here if you need anything. You are a very good manager and I have heard great things from the other project team members, both on your work on the project and your use of project management in your daily life," he told her.

Ashley was pleased with the praise from Thomas Robert Morgan. He was an icon in the industry and this was the smoothest-running project she had ever worked on. "I greatly appreciate your feedback," she told him sincerely. "When I first started this project, I felt like juggling two offices and my daily schedule would be too much. Your advice to apply project management to my life was so simple, but so insightful. Now, I am feeling less stressed than I have in years," she confessed.

Mr. Morgan laughed. "I have worked in this industry for *years*. I have seen a lot of professionals struggle in their daily lives, because they don't apply the same simple techniques to their personal lives that they do their work lives." He paused for a second. "Rarely have I seen someone understand how to apply project-management principles to their lives and embrace them so quickly. I am impressed, Ashley."

"I owe it to you," she told him. "Who knew that your email signature block would change my life?"

"Speaking of change," Mr. Morgan responded, "have you thought about how you will address change management in your daily life?"

This caught Ashley off guard. Of course scope change had been something that had been a focus since the kickoff meeting, but she hadn't considered this for her personal life. Now, it was time to start examining another aspect of project management and how it would apply to her personal life as a project.

"I hadn't thought about it," she confessed. "I was able to make adjustments for the holidays, but next year, I guess that will just be part of my normal planning."

"I'm here to assist if you need me," he told her. "I'm sure you have discovered that most of the project team is also available."

*__Change__ is inevitable and accelerating. Individuals who manage it effectively will be more successful and have less stress. Change initiatives are time consuming and costly, but by approaching change management with a disciplined approach, individuals can survive and thrive.*

That afternoon as Ashley drove to the gym, thoughts about change management and how she could develop a process that might work for her filled her head. Now that she had moved, she needed to consider what changes needed to occur in her life and whether they would impact her larger project scope. As Mr. Morgan always pointed out, projects went off track when there were changes that were not included in the change management process. She needed to develop a change management process for her own life. She realized change wasn't bad, just a necessary part of life. However, if she didn't track it, she would just end up in the same place as she had been when she started projectizing her life.

She considered what Jim had told her when she asked him about the changes to the project and the original design. The key had been to meticulously document the details and lock down the initial design. Getting that right would then allow for minimal change. How could she apply this to her personal life? She needed to scope her life well enough to allow normal activities and routines to have flexibility while at the same time clearly ensuring that the cost, time, and value of her life were balanced.

She realized a way to do this was by using a modified form of tracking cost and schedule variance. For projects, cost and schedule variance were tracked by strict mathematical formulas. She needed to develop a way to track significant changes and adjust as needed. Because she planned to apply to Project Management Master's Degree programs once the smart building project was finished, she knew project change was on the horizon.

That night, she examined her current budget and schedule. She decided that once a quarter or when a significant event occurred in her life, she would review. Anything that created more than 5% variance in time or cost would be considered a significant change and she would need to adjust the rest of her plans accordingly.

The next time she saw Thomas Robert Morgan, she told him.

"That's great news," he said. "I have another question that I wanted to ask you and that is why I wanted you to consider change management first."

"Sure," Ashley responded.

"This project will be wrapping up in about two months and when that time comes, I will be moving on to my next project. My next project will be in Seattle." He let Ashley process that a moment. "It would be great to have you as part of my team. I don't want you to decide right now. Give me an answer on Monday."

Ashley stood in the hallway, speechless. This was a dream opportunity, but there was so much to think about. This is where her family lived, she had just moved to a new townhouse, and she was researching master's degree programs.

# THE
# DECISION

THAT WEEKEND, ASHLEY STRUGGLED WITH the
difficult decision that was in front of her. She of course
discussed it with her mother and sister. They both wanted her to stay, but also knew she had to do what was best
for her career. She knew before she consulted with them
that they would stay as neutral as possible.

After leaving her mom and sister after mass, she needed to drop by her InTech office to look at some files on her position agreement with InTech. She went into her office and reviewed her conditions of employment. It was clear that she could easily resign with two weeks' notice and that she would make significantly more money by working on the next project with Thomas Robert Morgan. In addition, the experience and reputation she would build for her career were without measure.

She had always enjoyed her position at InTech and even while working on the smart building, she had made an effort to come by InTech at least twice a week. As she sat at her desk creating a pros-and-cons list of taking the job offer, Mark came by.

"What are you doing here on a Sunday?" she asked, startled.

"I left my laptop and am doing a site survey in Aspen tomorrow. I figured I would grab it now, instead of fighting traffic in the morning. Why are you here?" Mark asked.

"Thomas Robert Morgan has offered me a position on his next project," she told him. "The position is in Seattle and I am not sure if I should take it or not. My family and my life are here. I am only just getting organized," she confided.

"Ashley," Mark said, "you have certainly grown a lot over the past year on the smart-building project. It has been great to see you flourish and you are an asset to the office. When you told Chris and me about life as a project, it made a lot of sense. I struggled with work–life balance for a long time."

"Thanks," Ashley said. "This is an extremely difficult decision."

"When looking at the triple constraint of cost, schedule, and value, value is always the most important of the three," Mark said. "I'll see you in a few days and hope to know what you decided."

As Mark walked away, she reflected on his words. Value. She didn't need to look at her priority list to know the first one: family. Her decision was made.

The next day, she told Thomas Robert Morgan that she appreciated his offer but that she couldn't accept it. She needed to live her life as a project, by the scope she had already set for herself. She enjoyed her career, but for her, family would always come first.

Thomas smiled. "I am glad to hear that you made this decision based on your life as a project. You have been one of my best pupils. I guess this is one of the few cases where I might regret teaching you so well."

# CLOSING THE SMART BUILDING PROJECT

---

**THE RIBBON-CUTTING CEREMONY FOR THE** new Denver smart building was bittersweet for Ashley. She looked around at the amazing people she had worked with over the past year. It was going to be hard to say goodbye. It was great to see the building finished, but hard to know that most of the team would be leaving and she might never see them again.

Troy was the first to approach her once the formalities were over and he gave her a big bear hug. Troy was by far one of the best construction managers she had ever worked with. "It has been terrific working with you this past year," he said gruffly, "both on the building and your life. Don't forget everything that you've learned with us."

"Don't worry," Terri said, walking over. "Ashley isn't like you. Instead of fighting everything, she has embraced it. I have never seen Thomas Robert Morgan so happy that someone turned down a job offer of his," she added, laughing.

Terri was the first Human Resources manager who also understood project management, in Ashley's experience.

"I'm really going to miss consulting with the two of you," Ashley told her two primary partners in projectizing her life.

"You are the IT lead," Troy said. "Can't you just create a chat area or something where we can stay in touch?"

"Great idea," Ashley said. "I could even create a communication management plan for us," she added with a smile.

"Thomas created a monster with you," Troy groaned, and laughed.

Jim Brown, the detail-focused architect, came up to the group. "It has been great working with you guys and I hope I wasn't that much of a prima donna."

"You have been delightful," Terri told him. "We'll miss you in Seattle, but I hear your next building will be in Houston?"

"That's correct," Jim said. "I wish Thomas Robert Morgan were going to be the project manager, though. After this experience, it will be difficult for any project manager to live up to his standards."

Jason Lee, the detail-focused contracting lead, approached the group. "It has been great working with everyone," Jason said with his naturally friendly smile. "Sorry to hear that you won't be coming to Seattle with us," Jason said, nodding toward Ashley and Jim.

Carl Nelson, who had turned out to be the most down-to-earth lawyer she had ever met, walked up to the group at that moment. "Looks like we are on an even split of who will be going to Seattle," he said.

Jason smiled. "I always miss you on projects where you aren't with us. It is hard to find a good lawyer."

"I know Justin Carrol, the lawyer in Seattle," Carl said. "And Thomas Robert Morgan has personally vouched for the project manager I will be working with here on my next project," Carl told him.

Terri smiled. "I will tell Mr. Morgan that our next project should be overseas, where we can include you on the team. This whole business of having to have passed the bar exam in different states to practice is always confusing to me," Terri said. "Figuring out whether you can be on the team or not is one the hardest things I have to research for HR."

"It's fine," Carl reassured her. "I like Denver and it is one of my favorite places to work. That is why Colorado is one of the three states where I have taken the bar exam. Three is enough for me," he added with a smile.

Ashley smiled at the group. Each member had become more than a coworker—a friend.

Thomas Robert Morgan was finally able to break away from everyone who wanted to congratulate him on the project's success. Under his leadership, the building had finished both on time and under budget. He delivered a building that was so advanced it was being lauded in all of the technical magazines and reviews.

"I would like to propose a toast," he said, walking up to the team with a waiter who handed out a round of drinks. After each of his direct reports accepted a drink, Thomas Robert Morgan raised his glass. "To a successful project and an amazing project team. May each of you continue your life as a project with the same level of success."

"Cheers" rang around in a chorus. Each of the project team members knew that whether they were continuing on with Thomas Robert Morgan or going a separate way, their lives had been changed.

As the ribbon-cutting ceremony was winding down, Ashley found Terri and Troy one more time to give them hugs. She promised to set up a chat room that was easy enough even for Troy to use.

"Ashley, do you have a minute?" Carl asked, catching up with her as she headed to the door.

"Sure," she said.

"Now that we aren't on the same project and we are both staying in Denver, I thought it might be nice to get a drink together sometime," he told her a little awkwardly.

"I would like that very much, Carl," she said without hesitation. A lawyer who was also a genuinely great guy. He had potential.

# THE
# NEXT PROJECT

ASHLEY FELT CONFIDENT IN HER decision to stay
with InTech and continue with her old team and position. It felt right to be working with Mark and Chris
full-time again and they made a great team. She even enjoyed returning to smaller IT integration projects. It had
been an amazing opportunity to work as part of a large
team on a project that lasted a year, but she found that
the smaller projects kept her imagination and creativi-
ty more engaged. She liked working on several projects
simultaneously and exploring the limits of integrating
technology into living spaces.

She completed her applications to a few Master in Project Management programs and decided to attend Boston University. She had heard about a professor there, Dr. Warburton, who was highly regarded by Mr. Morgan. He had even coauthored the book, *The Art and Science of Project Management*, which Mr. Morgan referred to in his project kickoff meeting. BU had a great online program that was affordable and flexible with her schedule. She determined that going back to school met her criteria for change management and adjusted other areas of her life as needed.

She continued to balance her life around the priorities she had set and the triple constraint, but somehow it still felt like something was missing. Before she met Thomas Robert Morgan, she used to stay up at night and feel overwhelmed by all the things she needed to accomplish. Now, she went to bed at night feeling good about what she had accomplished and optimistic about her future. She also had seen how project management had helped her own family and some of her friends.

The next morning, she sent an email to Thomas Robert Morgan and received an immediate reply.

"Yes."

She spent a lot of time making plans after that email from Mr. Morgan. She decided that she needed to initiate a new project with people who were project managers and would easily understand Thomas Robert Morgan's message. Also, she wanted to initiate her first project with a small organization that would not be too intimidating to her. She reached out to the Pikes Peak Regional Chapter (PPRC) of the Project Management Institute and sent them her speaking proposal. They liked her idea and scheduled her to speak in just two months.

Ashley was nervous as she rode with Carl down to the PPRC meeting in Colorado Springs. When she told him about her presentation idea, he had gladly agreed to drive the almost two hours, because she was both very excited and nervous. It would also help to have a friendly face in the crowd.

As Ashley stood in front of the members of the PPRC, her hands trembled. Some people said that public speaking was ranked above dying as things people feared most. Ashley could understand it at that moment.

*Have you ever wondered what the key to life is? If one really existed. I know the answer and would like to share it with you today. My old boss, Thomas Robert Morgan, showed it to me, and he discovered it in the most unlikely of places.*

*The Project Management Institute is the largest project-management organization in the world.*

*The definition of a project is an endeavor to create a unique product, service, or result.*

*Every project has a beginning and an end.*

*Every life has a beginning and an end.*

*Every project is unique.*

*Each one of you is unique.*

*That's right. By definition, 'Life is a Project.'*

*I am passionate about project management and after tonight's talk, I know you will be, too.*

*In our day-to-day lives, we have a lot of activities and busy schedules.*

*By 'projectizing' your lifestyle, you will be better prepared for life's many challenges . . .*

After her presentation was over, she received a standing ovation from the PPRC members. She felt invigorated and knew that this was just the beginning of her next life's project.

# REFERENCES

*The 7 Habits of Highly Effective People*
by Stephen R. Covey

*Leading Change*
by John P. Kotter

*The Art and Science of Project Management*
by Roger Warburton and Vijay Kanabar

*A Guide to the Project Management
Body of Knowledge (PMBOK® Guide)*
by The Project Management Institute

# PROJECT MANAGEMENT TEMPLATES AVAILABLE AT AMYSHAMILTON.COM

---

**Change Management in Three Steps**

**Communications Management Plan**

**How to Create a Work Breakdown Structure**

**Project Plan**

**Risk Log**

**Risk Matrix**

**Scope Statement**

**& more...**

# ABOUT THE AUTHOR

AMY S. HAMILTON IS AN author, project manager, college professor, motivational speaker, and shoe aficionado. She became a certified Project Management Professional through the Project Management Institute in 2007 and has been a volunteer in her local chapters in Stuttgart, Germany, and Colorado Springs, CO. She presented on "The Secret to Life from a PMP" at TEDxStuttgart in September 2016 (http://www.amyshamilton.com/books).

She taught Project Management Tools at Colorado Technical University and was a facilitator for the Master's Degree Program in Project Management for Boston University.

Amy holds a Bachelor of Science (BS) in Geography from Eastern Michigan University, a Master of Science (MS) in Urban Studies from Georgia State University, Master in Computer Science (MSc) from the University of Liverpool, Master Certificates in Project Management (PM) and Chief Information Officer (CIO) from the National Defense University, and completed the US Air University, Air War College.

She is an award-winning public speaker and has presented in over twenty countries on overcoming adversity, reaching one's dreams, computer security, and project management.

She served in the Michigan Army National Guard as a communications specialist and was commissioned into the US Army Officer Signal Corp, serving on Active Duty and later the US Army Reserves. She has worked at the US European Command, the US Northern Command, and North American Aerospace Defense Command (NORAD) on multiple communications and IT projects.

Amy is a woman who is passionate about project management, public speaking, and shoes.

# LEARN MORE AT
### *amyshamilton.com*

I am passionate about public speaking, project management, & shoes

Made in the USA
Columbia, SC
07 May 2017